T0143930

Spiritual Warfare Prayer

BY
DOROTHY WOODS

To order additional copies of this book, contact:
Xlibris
1-888-795-4274
www.Xlibris.com
Orders@Xlibris.com

Heavenly Father, I praise You and thank You and rejoice in Your presence. I glorify Your Name. Thank You, of Lord, for saving me and giving me new life in Jesus Christ. (II Corinthians 4:16)

I surrender to You that Your perfect will be done in me and through me to Your highest pleasure. (Revelations 4:11)

I pray for those who have done anything against me (name them). I lift them up that You may bless them and minister to their needs. I forgive them and ask You to forgive them also. And forgive me of my sins and let my transgressions be removed from me "as far as the east is from the west" (Psalms 103:12)

Thank You for Your kindness and mercy to me and also to those who have hurt me and done all matter of evil against me. I pray for their deliverance as well as my own.

I come to You freely and with confidence by the blood of Jesus (Hebrew 10:10, Amp.) which covers me and washes me, clean, body, mind, soul, and spirit, that my presence before You may be holy and my prayers upright and effective in You. For "thou, oh Lord, art a shield for me, my glory, and the lifter of mine head". (Psalms3: 3)

And I praise you, Father, with head lifted up, that You "teach my hands to war, and my fingers to fight" (Psalms 144:1) that I may "execute vengeance upon the heathen" (Psalms149: 7) and drive out all iniquity from the land. (Numbers 33:52) For "the fear of the Lord is to hate evil. (Proverbs 8:13) And Your determination is to destroy the works of the devil (I John 3:8)

Glory to God: because You have shown me that my warfare is not with flesh and blood but against principalities and powers, rulers of the darkness of this world and spiritual wickedness in high places (Ephesians 6:12)

Therefore, in the name of Jesus, I take authority over serpents and scorpions and over all the power of the enemy. (Luke 10:19) I tie up, bind, chain, forbid and cast out both in me and also before me (Matthews 16:23 & 18:18) the spirits of pride, fear, poverty, lust, bitterness, resentment, anger, selfishness, haughtiness, arrogance, jealousy, lying, false spiritual gifts, false fruit of the spirit, laziness, sluggishness, sneakiness, guile, deceptions, loss of memory, mind control, witchcrafts, automatic writings an etchings, divinations, occultism, wicked imaginations, unbelief, unclean dreams and fantasies, violence, false judgment, false anointing, bigotry, rejection, murder, rebellion, self righteousness and all related and associated demons and all spirits not of the kingdom of God.

By the power of the Holy Spirit I release the seven spirit of God upon me, the spirit of Jehovah. The spirit of wisdom and understanding. The spirit of counselor and might. The spirit of knowledge, and the spirit of the fear of God. (Isaiah 11:2)

I also invoke the commanding spirits upon me.

A NEW SPIRIT!

THE SPIRIT OF SONSHIP!

THE SPIRIT OF JEHOVAH!

THE SPIRIT OF GOD'S SON JESUS!

THE SPIRIT OF GRACE!

THE SPIRIT OF GLORY!

THE SPIRIT OF PROSPERITY!

THE SPIRIT OF FAITH!

THE SPIRIT OF REVELATION!

THE SPIRIT OF PROPHECY!

THE SPIRIT OF FORGIVING!

THE SPIRIT OF GIVING!

THE SPIRIT OF TRUSTING IN THE LORD!

THE SPIRIT OF TRUTH!

THE SPIRIT OF POWER, LOVE, AND SOUND MIND!

THE SPIRIT OF HOLINESS!

I also break, sever, and cast off all curses of any form or nature placed upon me, my family, and friends by wicked spirits and their human agents; and ask You, Lord, to return them back to their sources. (Genesis 27:29 & Deuteronomy 30:7 & Psalms 109:17-19)

"Let the arms of the wicked be broken, Oh God". (Psalms 37:17) "Let them consume into smoke" (Psalms 37:20)

"Fight against them that fight against me" (Psalms 35:1)

Let them be confounded and put to shame that seek after my soul to destroy it. Let them be driven backward and put to shame that wish me evil. (Psalms 40:14) Let their way be dark and slippery and let the Angel of the Lord persecute them.

"When I cry unto thee, then shall mine enemies turn back; this I know, for God is with me" (Psalms 56:9)

Let evil slay the wicked; and them that hate me be made desolate (Psalms 43:1)

In God I boast all the day long and praise thy name forever. (Psalms 44:8) For You have delivered my soul in peace from the battle that was against me. (Psalms 55:18) "Let all that seek thee rejoice and be glad in thee: let such as love thy salvation say continually, the LORD be magnified." (Psalms 40:16) For "the enemies of God's people shall be scattered and them that hate us shall flee before us" (Numbers 10:35)

Let them be confounded and consumed that are adversaries to my soul; let them be covered with reproach and dishonor that seek my hurt. But I will hope continually, and will yet praise thee more and more. My mouth shall shew forth thy righteousness and thy salvation all the day. I will go in the strength of the LORD MY GOD (Psalms 71:13-16)

So "arise, OH LORD, in thine anger, lift up thyself because of the rage of mine enemies and awake for me to the judgment that thou hast commanded." (Psalms 7:6)

Bring your vengeance upon my enemies. Let the hornets of the Lord (Exodus 23:28) scatter the spirits of poverty and family destroying spirits and all demons risen up against me, my family and friends. Case them, Oh God, "until they that are left and hide themselves be destroyed". (Deuteronomy 7:20) And let my cup of blessing (Psalms 23:5) run over with joy and blessing, goodness and power, peace and prosperity through Jesus Christ, my Lord. (Ephesians 1:3 & Deuteronomy 28:1-14) And let all that has been taken from me be restored unto me seven fold. (Proverbs 6:31)

"Let overflowing hailstones and stormy wind come against all lying and deceptive spirits who would speak lies to me and who would speak lies about me to others (Ezekiel 38:22) Destroy, Oh LORD, and divide their tongues: for I have seen violence and strife in the city (Psalms 55:9)

Let the Spirit of the Fear of the Lord rise up against wickedness and rebellion against God, both in me and also before. Through love's perfect power I resist, reject and cast out all fear, intimidation, nervousness, fret and all related spirits from my family, my friends, and myself. (I John. 4:18) And I praise You, heavenly Father, for Your own love which flows in our hearts, minds and souls toward you and toward our neighbors. (Matthew 22:37-40)

I plead the Blood of Jesus against the prince the prince of darkness assigned against my church, (name your church.) I forbid Satan and his demons from hindering or interfering in any way with God's work. "Rain upon him and upon his bands and many that are with him an overflowing rain and great hailstones of fire and brimstone (Ezekiel 38:22)

Unto all murderous and destructive spirits let the Slayer and Revenger of blood (Numbers 35:19-25) pursue (Deuteronomy 19:6) them until their blood also is shed and the land is made them clean. (Numbers 35:33)

Upon all tormenting spirits, headache demons and spirits of infirmity, discouragement and confusion I loose the anger and finger of God. (Luke 11:20) "Draw out also the spear, and stop the way against them that persecute me." (Psalms 35:3) Let the Spirit of Peace deliver peace unto me and comfort; and let the Lord, with healing in his wings, alight upon me with virtue and power (Mark 5:25-30) and bring restoration to my soul and body (Psalms 23:3) through Jesus Christ, my Lord.

Father, use me to glorify You and to cause many to glorify Your Name. "For with thee is the fountain of life; in thy light shall we see light." (Psalms 36:3)

Bring down, Oh God, the strongholds of darkness which have risen up against me, my home, my church, my ministry, and my work; and let the arrows of the enemy be shattered to pieces. Let the Word of God go forth to cause the bow of Satan to be smitten out of his hand and his arrows to fall our of his right hand (Ezekiel 39:3)

I exalt You, Oh LORD, forevermore! May Your Name be magnified in the midst of Your church and they pollute it no more, And the heathen will know You are the Lord, the Holy one. (Ezekiel 39:7)

And I appropriate the Blood of Jesus. (Leviticus 16:6) I receive it upon my head and upon my heart, upon my mind, and my soul, my flesh, and my family, (Hebrew 9:22) and all things used for my ministry and my church (name your church) (Hebrew 9:21) I receive now all that the Blood of Jesus provides for me. And I plead the Blood against all that the devil would try to bring against me or destroy or kill or steal from me.

Let the Blood of Christ cry out (Genesis 4:10) against the evil and wickedness the devil has brought against me and let it preserve me from all the wickedness, which the devil has planned. And let the grace of my God be bestowed upon me richly and abundantly in all wisdom and knowledge, power and understanding, through Jesus Christ my Lord.

Praise You for Your goodness and grace, Oh Lord, my Strength and my Redeemer. Let me be strong in You and in the power of Your MIGHT (Ephesians 6:10) Let the fruit of Your Spirit (Galatians 5:22) increase and abound in my soul; and may each gift of the Spirit be administered unto me freely as the need arises. (I Corinthians 12:4-11)

Let me increase in favor with God and with man, that I may receive Your highest pleasure, guarding and keeping my heart with all diligence, knowing that out of it comes the issues of life (Proverbs 4:23)

In Perfect humility let me be an epistle read of all men (II Corinthians 3:2) For I desire the Word of Christ to dwell in me richly (Colossians 3:16) and for Jesus to be manifest in and through me in thought, word, and deed.

Lead me always in the Way of righteousness that I walk not after the flesh but after the Spirit. (Romans 8:1)

Let me be a blessing to others wherever I go and wherever I am.

IN JESUS' NAME AMEN!

Printed in the United States
By Bookmasters